Standardization Toolkit

A Reference Guide for National Statistical Systems

Doreen Ninsiima Kasozi

Preamble

Standardization in National Statistical Systems (NSSs) is fast becoming an important domain. The accumulative prominence of evidence based approaches to inform national and global development initiatives, emphasize the need for production of high quality statistics. Overtime, statistical data collection and reporting has been conducted to suit the needs of individual policy initiatives, following the ebb and flow of economic concerns. However, in recent years, statistical organizations realized the need to not only strengthen statistical capacities through strategic planning, but also develop and implement standards to enhance quality, commonality, comparability, and interchangeability in statistical development. Subsequently, standardization was purposefully introduced and championed globally as an antecedent for quality control, assessment, auditing and certification of official statistics. The Standardization toolkit has been designed for National Statistical Systems as a reference guide on the conceptualization, development, implementation and actualization of standards. The toolkit uncovers vital roles standards play in modern society and details procedures undertaken in developing and implementing standards for statistics. The toolkit is applicable, based on sound principles. It is essential for sectoral, national and regional statistical systems, researchers in academic and scientific fields, as well as practitioners responsible for standardization programmes as they identify and make informed choices about standardization opportunities within their own organizations.

About the Author

Dr Doreen Ninsiima Kasozi is a Quality Compliance Expert, Leader and Trainer. With over a decade of work experience in quality assurance, standardization, consulting and advisory in strategic management, she has maintained a track record of building professional teams in statistical quality. She began her literary life as an academic researcher publishing research papers on Quality Compliance, Organizational Performance in Business Organizations, Quality Assurance and Statistical Use in Africa, Public Sector Innovation and Business Process Reengineering with; the International Journal for Quality Assurance and Management, the International Journal of Science and Engineering Research and the International Journal of Business and Management respectively. Through her expertise, statistical specialists in Government line Ministries, Departments and Agencies in Uganda's National System were trained in key quality management concepts, quality assurance, and auditing and standards implementation.

Dr Doreen has also presented at regional and international forums to various professional groups. Most notably on Statistical Confidentiality and Disclosure Control at the Nigeria Statistical Office, Statistical User Engagement practices in Addis Ababa, Ethiopia and Promoting Statistical Data Quality at the Data Governance and Information Quality Conference in San Diego, USA. Throughout her quality compliance career, Doreen has preserved her passion and excitement for quality management work both nationally and internationally, even more so now as quality becomes a priority strategic option for many business organizations. She is a fundamentalist when it comes to writing, and always looks forward to providing guidance to upcoming researchers in the quality management and business space.

Contents

1.   Introduction

Standards have become central building blocks on the road to worldwide consensus among technology, industry and society. Internationally, the United Nations (UN) and the Economic Commission for Europe (ECE) adopted a set of "Fundamental Principles of Official Statistics." Included among the 10 principles were calls for statistical organizations to use professional standards based on scientific principles to guide the methods and procedures for the collection, processing, storage, and presentation of statistical data. The principles also called for the inclusion of relevant information on the sources, methods, and procedures of the statistics.

Similarly, the International Organization for Standardization (ISO), which is responsible for promoting standardization throughout the World develops and disseminates standards in collaboration with IEC (International Electro technical Commission), to Government and Private Agencies under the Worldwide Federation of National Standards, for implementation in their respective Countries.

The National Statistical System (NSS) is an ensemble of statistical organisations and units within a country that jointly collect process and disseminate official statistics. In a given country, the leading statistical agency is often referred to as the National Statistical Office (OECD, 2002). One of the primary benefits for standardization in a National Statistical System is a synchronized quality assured end to end process.

This would facilitate;

i.   Reduced process variations;
ii. minimal duplication of production efforts and cost Reduction in time and resources;
iii. Effective inter-temporal coherence and comparability of statistics; and
iv. Consistency in the use of names and definitions for populations, statistical units, concepts, variables, and classifications across and within statistical systems/programmes/domains.

The outcomes of standardized systems are linked to dependable efficiency gains and sustained quality improvements

2. Standardization Concept and Structure

In social sciences and economics, the idea of standardization is close to the solution for a coordination problem, a situation in which all parties can realize mutual gains, but only by making mutually consistent decisions (Blind, 2004). From statistical perspective, it expedites development and Implementation of concepts, doctrines, classifications, procedures and designs to achieve the required levels of compatibility, Quality, commonality or interchangeability in all operational, technical, production and administrative fields of society.

2.1 Notional Outlook

Standardization is the process of developing and implementing technical standards based on consensus of different parties that include firms, users, interest groups, standards organizations and governments (Zongjie, Hall, McCarthy, Skitmore, & Shen, 2016), while a *Standard* is defined as *"a document established by consensus and approved by a recognized body that provides for common and repeated use, rules, guidelines or characteristics for activities or their results, aimed at the achievement of the optimum degree of order in a given context"* (ISO/IEC Guide 2:1996).

Standardization maximizes compatibility, interoperability, safety, repeatability, or excellence. It facilitates commoditization of formerly custom processes. Through this process, different types of standards emerge and are adopted for use. Standardization follows a consensus-based approach in developing standards worldwide. With this approach, either closed or full consensus processes are undertaken to produce standards. The closed consensus process is characterised by restricted membership and formal procedures, for due-process among voting members, while the full consensus process is often open to all interested, qualified parties, with formal procedures for due-process considerations. Both closed and full consensus processes are used by Standards Organisations (ISO/IEC Guide 2:1996; ISO, 2016). Generally, standards serve as a tool for exchange and collaboration. They are very valuable in environments where different entities collaborate. Standards provide a necessary foundation for exchangeability of production means among statistics producers. (Braaksma, Colasanti, Falorsi, Kloek, Miguelangel, Vidal, Museux, Szep, 2013). However, the existence of a published standard does not necessarily imply that it is useful or correct. Just because an item is stamped with a standard number does not, by itself, indicate that the item is fit for any particular use. The folks who use the item or service (engineers, trade unions, etc.) or specify it (building codes, government, industry, etc.) have a responsibility to consider the available standards, specify the correct one, enforce compliance, and use the item correctly.

Historical Context…..

Standards are off springs of the Industrial Age. Their implementation became highly important with the onset of the Industrial Revolution and the need for high-precision machine tools and interchangeable parts in industry and commerce. Henry Maudslay developed the first industrially practical screw-cutting lathe in 1800. This allowed for the standardization of screw thread sizes for the first time and paved the way for the practical application of interchangeability (an idea that was already taking hold) to nuts and bolts (Ping, 2011) Before this, screw threads were usually made by chipping and filing (that is, with skilled freehand use of chisels and files). Nuts were rare; metal screws, when made at all, were usually for use in wood. Metal bolts passing through wood framing to a metal fastening on the other side were usually fastened in non-threaded ways (such as clinching or upsetting against a washer). Maudslay standardized the screw threads used in his workshop and produced sets of taps and dies that would make nuts and bolts consistently to those standards, so that any bolt of the appropriate size would fit any nut of the same size. This was a major advance in workshop technology (Rolt, 1962). Maudslay's work, as well as the contributions of other engineers, accomplished a modest amount of industry standardization; some companies' in-house standards spread a bit within their industries.

Joseph Whitworth's screw thread measurements were adopted as the first (unofficial) national standard by companies around the country in 1841. It came to be known as the British Standard Whitworth, and was widely adopted in other countries (Gilbert & Galloway, 1978; Lee,1900). This new standard specified a 55° thread angle and a thread depth of 0.640327p and a radius of 0.137329p, where p is the pitch. The thread pitch increased with diameter in steps specified on a chart. An example of the use of the Whitworth thread is the Royal Navy's Crimean War gunboats. These were the first instance of "mass-production" techniques being applied to marine engineering (Ping, 2011). With the adoption of BSW by British railway lines, many of which had previously used their own standard both for threads and for bolt head and nut profiles, and improving manufacturing techniques, it came to dominate British manufacturing. American Unified Coarse was originally based on almost the same imperial fractions. The Unified thread angle is 60° and has flattened crests (Whitworth crests are rounded). Thread pitch is the same in both systems except that the thread pitch for the 1/2 in bolt is 12 threads per inch (tpi) in BSW versus 13 tpi in the UNC. By the end of the 19th century, differences in standards between companies, was making trade increasingly difficult and strained. For instance, an iron and steel dealer recorded his displeasure in The Times: "Architects and engineers generally specify such unnecessarily diverse types of sectional material or given work that anything like economical and continuous manufacture becomes impossible. In this country no two professional men are agreed upon the size and weight of a girder to employ for given work."

The Engineering Standards Committee was established in London in 1901 as the world's first national standards body (McWilliam & Robert, 2001; BSI, 2010) It subsequently extended its standardization work and became the British Engineering Standards Association in 1918, adopting the name British Standards Institution in 1931 after receiving its Royal Charter in 1929. The national standards were adopted universally throughout the country, and enabled the markets to act more rationally and efficiently, with an increased level of cooperation. After the First World War, similar national bodies were established in other countries. The Deutsches Institut für Normung was set up in Germany in 1917, followed by its counterparts, the American National Standard Institute and the French Commission Permanente de Standardization, both in 1918 (Ping, 2011).

By the mid to late 19th century, efforts were being made to standardize electrical measurement. Lord Kelvin was an important figure in this process, introducing accurate methods and apparatus for measuring electricity. In 1857, he introduced a series of effective instruments, including the quadrant electrometer, which cover the entire field of electrostatic measurement. He invented the current balance, also known as the Kelvin balance or Ampere balance (SiC), for the precise specification of the ampere, the standard unit of electric current (Lindley, 2005). R. E. B. Crompton drew up the first international standards body, the International Electrotechnical Commission, in 1906.

Another important figure was R. E. B. Crompton, who became concerned by the large range of different standards and systems used by electrical engineering companies and scientists in the early 20th century. Many companies had entered the market in the 1890s and all chose their own settings for voltage, frequency, current and even the symbols used on circuit diagrams. Adjacent buildings would have totally incompatible electrical systems simply because they had been fitted out by different companies. Crompton could see the lack of efficiency in this system and began to consider proposals for an international standard for electric engineering (Fray, 2010). In 1904, Crompton represented Britain at the International Electrical Congress, held in connection with Louisiana Purchase Exposition in Saint Louis as part of a delegation by the Institute of Electrical Engineers. He presented a paper on standardization, which was so well received that he was asked to look into the formation of a commission to oversee the process (Johnson & Randell, 1948). By 1906 his work was complete and he drew up a permanent constitution for the first international standards organization, the International Electrotechnical Commission (Dyer, Moseley, Ogumi, Rand, & Scrosati, 2010).

The primary effect of standardization on organizations is that the basis of competition is shifted from integrated systems to individual components within the system. Prior to standardization, an organization's product must span the entire system because individual components from different competitors are incompatible, but after standardization each company can focus on providing an individual component of the system (Shapiro, Carl &Varian, 1999). When the shift toward competition based on individual components takes place, organizations selling tightly integrated systems must quickly shift to a modular approach, supplying other companies with subsystems or components (Christensen & Raynor, 2003).

Standardization has a variety of opportunities for consumers, including enhanced network effects. Standards increase interoperability between products, allowing information to be shared within a larger network and attracting more consumers to use the new technology, further enhancing network effects. Other standardization opportunities to consumers are reduced uncertainty, because consumers can be more certain that they are not choosing the wrong product, and reduced lock-in, because the standard makes it more likely that there will be competing products in the space. Consumers may also get the benefit of being able to mix and match components of a system to align with their specific preferences (Shapiro, Carl &Varian, 1999). Once these initial outcomes of standardization are realized, further prospects that accrue to consumers as a result of using the standard are driven mostly by the quality of the technologies underlying that standard (Sidak, 2016).

Probably the greatest downside of standardization for consumers is lack of variety. There is no guarantee that the chosen standard will meet all consumers' needs or even that the standard is the best available option. Another downside is that if a standard is agreed upon before products are available in the market, then consumers are deprived of the penetration pricing that often results when rivals are competing to rapidly increase market share in an attempt to increase the likelihood that their product will become the standard (Shapiro, Carl &Varian, 1999). It is also possible that a consumer will choose a product based upon a standard that fails to become dominant (Cowan,1991). In this case, the consumer will have spent resources on a product that is ultimately less useful to him or her as the result of the standardization process. Standardization is implemented significantly when organizations release new products to market. Compatibility is important for products to be successful; this allows consumers to use their new items along with what they already own.

2.2   Guiding principles for Standardization

Four guiding principles that underlie standardization are:

i.   Openness and transparency of the process

Transparency is critical in the preparation of Standards. Transparency means that every act must follow a well-established procedure; that the procedure is equitable to all parties; and that each step in the standards development process is open and available for scrutiny.

ii. **Consensus**

Consensus in standards development is the process through which a Technical Committee, consisting of many different and sometimes opposed interests, arrives at a general agreement on the content and requirements of a Standard. This produces a Standard which best matches the needs and values of our society as a whole, and due to representation of a range of parties, broad community acceptance is assured.

iii. **Balance of representation**

The membership of a Standards Committee should be representative of key stakeholders to cover a wide spectrum of their interests.

2.3 Categorization of Standards

There four broad categories of standards (ISO, 2016) widel used. Where applicable, these are discussed with some examples of statistical standards within the categories.

i. *De facto standards*

These are standards followed by informal convention or dominant usage. A de facto standard is a custom, convention, product, or system that has achieved a dominant position by public acceptance or market forces (such as early entrance to the market). De facto is a Latin phrase meaning "concerning the fact" or "in practice". *An example of a De facto statistical standard is the UN Fundamental Principles of Official Statistics (Annex D)*

ii. ***De jure standards***

These are standards which are part of legally binding contracts, laws or regulations. De jure (in Latin de iure) is an expression that means *"concerning law"*, as opposed to de facto, which means *"concerning fact"*. The terms de jure and de facto are used instead of "in law" and "in practice", respectively, when one is describing political or legal situations. *Some examples within a statistical context include National Statistical Policies, Memoranda of Understanding between two or more Statistical Organizations.*

iii. ***Voluntary standards***

These are standards published and made available for people to consider for use. In social sciences, a voluntary standard that is also a de facto standard is a typical solution n to a coordination problem (Ullmann-Margalit , 2015). The choice of a de facto standard is the better choice for situations in which all parties can realize mutual gains, but only by making mutually consistent decisions.

iv. ***Technical Standards***

A Technical standard is an established norm or requirement about technical systems. It is usually a formal document that establishes uniform engineering or technical criteria, methods, processes and practices.

Examples include the ISO 9000 family of quality management systems standards, ISO 9001:2015 – Quality Management Systems, ISO 13053-1:2011(Quantitative methods in process improvement -- Six Sigma-Part 1: DMAIC methodology), International Standard on Quality Control (ISQC), ISO 9004:2009 (A quality management approach).

In statistical production and management, examples of the latest editions of technical standards include;

- The SNA- System of National Accounts Standard for compilation of National Accounts (United Nations, 2008a).

- The ISIC- International Standard Industrial Classification of All Economic Activities (ISIC) used as an international reference classification for productive activities in statistics compilation (United Nations, 2008b).

- The CPC- Central Product Classification which constitutes a comprehensive classification of all products, including goods and services used in statistics compilation. CPC presents categories for all products that can be the object of domestic or international transactions or that can be entered into stocks (United Nations, 2015).

- The COICOP - Classification of Individual Consumption According to Purpose is an integral part of the SNA, but it is also intended for use in three other statistical areas: household budget surveys, consumer price indices and international comparisons of gross domestic product (GDP) and its component expenditures (United Nations, 2000).

- The HS - Harmonized Commodity Description and Coding System, also known as the Harmonized System (HS) of tariff nomenclature is an internationally standardized system of names and numbers to classify traded products (United Nations, 2017).

- The ISCED- the International Standard Classification of Education provides a comprehensive framework for organizing education programmes and qualification by applying uniform and internationally agreed definitions to facilitate comparisons of education systems across countries (UNESCO, 2011). It is a reference standard in the compilation of education statistics.

- GFS Manual- Government Finance Statistics Manual describes an integrated Government Finance Statistics (GFS) system that is harmonized, to the extent possible. It is designed to support compilation of Government Finance Statistics (IMF, 2014).

- The ISCO- International Standard Classification of Occupations (ISCO) is an International Labour Organization (ILO) classification structure for organizing information on labour and jobs (ILO, 2012). It is used in the compilation of labour related statistics.

2.4   Stages in Standards Development

Development of standards follows a systematic, comprehensive and consensus based approach. The following stages are undertaken in developing standards;

i.   Needs identification for a specific standard required

ii.   Drafting a proposal for the standard that will be developed, providing sufficient detail to evaluate the proposal- but not too elaborate, and documenting the draft using a standard template.

iii.   Undertake a Proposal assessment. The urgency, complexity, existing candidates, and user base for the specific should be established. If they exist, determine the user needs through profiling them and assessing planned resource costs (time & resources) and technical content.

iv.   Get buy-in from stakeholders through bilateral consultations, stakeholder workshops and meetings. Then gather comments for final stakeholder approval.

v.   Edit the standard. This involves consolidating comments into a comments log, incorporating the comments into the draft standard and documenting responses.

vi.   Test the standard: No matter how well the standard is written, there will be problems when it is actually used. Examine and/or pilot before formal approval.

vii. Get formal approval of the standard: Once consensus has been achieved, approve the timetable for implementation.

viii. Disseminate and Publish the Standard: Once the standard has been approved for adoption and implementation, it should be widely disseminated and then published.

ix.   Training: Deliberate organizational plans for standards training should be considered (courses training and sharing promotional material for the standard are key)

x.   Implement and use the standard (Clear action plans for implementation of the standard across the organization/s)

xi.   Assess the use and effectiveness of standard: (Evaluation studies and compliance monitoring on the extent to which the standard is used are key). A Gap analysis is also considered to identify any problem areas of the organization's management systems and procedures in meeting the requirements of the developed standard.

xii. Review standard periodically, Retain (if unchanged), revise or retire (superseded, etc)

2.5   Standards Implementation

When standards are developed and approved, they are ready for use. To guide standards implementation, an action plan should be designed with clear implementation strategies, outputs and procedures on how the standards will be used. The plan should define the implementation structure including the roles, functions, deliverables and collaborations of all stakeholders involved in implementing the standards. A uniform reporting mechanism should also be adopted for regular progress reporting on standards implementation, identifying non-conformance & preventive action and adherence to internationally recommended standards and best practices. Key implementation strategies including; advocacy, stakeholder engagement, and training on the application of standards, Documentation of standards and related concepts, processes, systems & outputs for statistical quality, Compliance monitoring and assessments of the effectiveness of the standards are crucial for implementation. The implementation plan (for example annual, bi-annual or five yearly), should include a detailed financing plan

2.6   Standards Revision

Standards are often revised every five years or more, to establish their technical, scientific and social validity, implementability, and auditability. For a given standard, a formal review procedure is implemented through independent structures that are guided by a set of core elements, which determine the criteria and outcome of the revision. These elements are therefore critical in determining the standards subjected to revision or modification within a specified period. They include;

i.   *Usefulness - Standards that allows a producer, user or statistical office evaluate compliance with a particular Indicator.*

ii. *Practicality - Clear, auditable standards that can be used to objectively assess the compliance of statistical management operations. Indicators should not: require special skills to measure; need complicated analysis; or, be expensive to measure.*

iii. *Merit – The standard must have scientific merit and socially validity.*

iv. *Consistent - Provisions of logical, coherent rationalization for regional variation and the ability for Certification Bodies to uniformly apply the standard.*

v.   *Understandable – The intent and performance of the standards should be easily communicable to diverse audiences.*

vi.   ***Comprehensive*** *– The standards must address the significant issues and demands required to ensure exemplary statistical production and management.*

vii.   ***Relevant*** *– The standards and indicators must be linked to stakeholder values.*

Figure 1. An illustration of the Standards Development, Implementation and Revision progressions

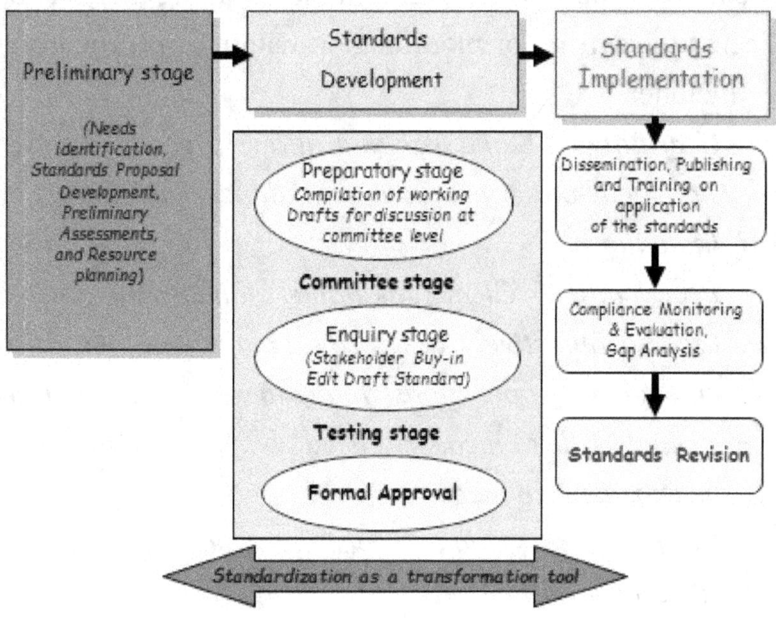

3.   Basic Techniques for Standardization

In determining the appropriate standardization technique for a given process or output, the respective statistics should be used by a representative group of key stakeholders – *statistics producers, and/or regulators;* it should be produced regularly, and should have been independently evaluated before. Statistics outputs that are not suitable for standardization are, either produced once, not frequent, or generated on a small scale to meet a specific need, for just that period of time. Standardization may not also apply where statistical methods, processes or protocols have not been validated or for which there is no interest in those particular statistical outputs by the stakeholder community. Before undertaking a standardization exercise, *verification and validation* is done to determine whether the statistical output is appropriate for standardization. In the standardization of production systems, 4 basic techniques are used to ensure quality outputs are achieved and maintained. These include; *simplification or variety control, codification, value engineering and statistical process control.* The most commonly used are *codification* especially, for improving and enhancing data management/ information systems, and *statistical process control* for ensuring statistical quality of various outputs.

3.1   Verification and validation

Verification is the evaluation of whether or not a product, service or system complies with a regulation, requirement, specification, or imposed condition (often an internal process) while validation is the assurance that a product, service or system meets the needs of the customer and other identified stakeholders. It involves acceptance and suitability with external customers (Project Management Institute, 2008; Project Management Institute, 2013). Before deciding to embark on a standardization process for a particular Statistics product, service or system, it is essential that the results for which the standard will be based are reproducible and repeatable, *i.e. give the same results, within statistical error, when repeated by a single user and by multiple users.* This does not mean that a full uncertainty budget should have been established but that there must be a high degree of confidence that the procedures to be standardized can be validated and the results obtained can be verified. When developing a standard, the scope of application is carefully evaluated, what is not covered is equally carefully defined, the procedures to be incorporated are carefully scrutinized by other experts to ensure that they are appropriate and cannot be misinterpreted, the terms and symbols used are accurately defined, any 'normative references', i.e. other standards that are critical to the application and operation of the new standard are identified, all statements are appropriately justified, normative and informative elements are differentiate, requirements for compliance with the standard are clearly stated, etc.

3.2 Simplification or variety control

This involves the use of similar approaches to apply to a wide range of production processes to ensure quality control. This is commonly used in manufacturing plants and factories. Development and implementation of uniform concepts, doctrines, procedures and designs to achieve and maintain the required levels of compatibility, interchangeability or commonality in operational, procedural, material, technical and administrative fields requires a simple technique with a wide range of control applications for standardization across the various production systems. As a standardization technique, it provides for;

- End-to-end" metadata systems development
- Harmonization of terminology, definitions, methods, and classifications
- Documentation and mapping statistical process descriptions
- Process-based organization structures

3.3 Value Engineering

This is an approach used to optimize project life cycle costs, save time, increase profits, improve quality, expand market share, solve problems and or use resources more effectively (Project Management Institute, 2008; Project Management Institute, 2013). The potential value of any statistical system is measured to determine its efficiency and effectiveness in production to deliver the desired statistical outputs, vs the actual outputs it generates. In order to standardize, a standard unit of measure, compilation method or weighting technique can be considered to derive the desired value of statistical production outputs, and improve appropriately, in cases where variations occur hence resulting in sub-standard statistical outputs.

3.4   Codification

This is a common statistical technique used to ensure coherence, consistency within and across various data sets, systems or domains, for uniform, harmonized and quality statistical outputs. Codification which is mainly used at the data processing stage is a quality control mechanism for ensuring that the fields, variables and units captured on a specific group or population match the original records. Unique identifiers for specific or related statistics, variables or fields are allocated for easy access or system retrieval. Statistical systems with standardized coding can be integrated and easily compared nationally, regionally and globally.

3.5   Statistical Process Control

Statistical Process Control (SPC) is one of the Total Quality Management (TQM) methods that improves quality and reduces variation. TQM is a continuous improvement process developed to satisfy the customers by meeting their expectations. The seven basic Quality Control tools that help eliminate randomness in a process include; the pareto diagram, process flow chart, cause and effect diagram, check sheet, histogram, scatter diagram and control chart (Mystica, Bai & Suganthi, 2015).

As a standardization technique, SPC involves systematic examination of specific parts of a process following a set of instructions that provide direction on process flow, in order to attain optimization and consistency of a desired statistical output. It provides for; uniform measurement of individual or integrated statistical system components or outputs, while ensuring that the process operates efficiently, producing more specification-conforming products with less waste (rework or scrap).

> ### *Historical Feature......*
>
> *SPC was pioneered by Walter A. Shewhart at Bell Laboratories in the early 1920s. He developed the control chart in 1924. Shewhart consulted with Colonel Leslie E. Simon in the application of control charts to munitions manufacture at the Army's Picatinny Arsenal in 1934. That successful application helped convince Army Ordnance to engage AT&T's George Edwards to consult on the use of statistical quality control among its divisions and contractors at the outbreak of World War II. W. Edwards Deming invited Shewhart to speak at the Graduate School of the U.S. Department of Agriculture. Deming was an important architect of the quality control short courses that trained American industry in the new techniques during WWII. Deming traveled to Japan during the Allied Occupation and met with the Union of Japanese Scientists and Engineers (JUSE) in an effort to introduce SPC methods to Japanese industry (Deming, 1950).*

Statistical process control (SPC) procedures help in monitoring process behavior. Arguably the most successful SPC tool is the control chart. A control chart helps record data and visualizes when an unusual event, e.g., a very high or low observation compared with "typical" process performance, occurs (Bower, 2018).

Control charts attempt to distinguish between two types of process variation:

- Common cause variation, which is intrinsic to the process and will always be present.
- Special cause variation, which stems from external sources and indicates that the process is out of statistical control.

Various tests can help determine when an out-of-control event has occurred. However, as more tests are employed, the probability of a false alarm also increases. Many SPC techniques have been "rediscovered" by American firms in recent years, especially as a component of quality improvement initiatives like Six Sigma. The widespread use of control charting procedures has been greatly assisted by statistical software packages and ever-more sophisticated data collection systems. Over time, other process-monitoring tools have been developed, including:

- Cumulative Sum (CUSUM) charts: the ordinate of each plotted point represents the algebraic sum of the previous ordinate and the most recent deviations from the target.
- Exponentially Weighted Moving Average (EWMA) charts: each chart point represents the weighted average of current and all previous subgroup values, giving more weight to recent process history and decreasing weights for older data.

More recently, others have advocated integrating SPC with Engineering Process Control (EPC) tools, which regularly change process inputs to improve performance (Bower, 2018).

4. Standards Documentation

Standards are developed using a rigorous and robust process, which includes detailed peer review at different stages, in order to ensure that users can have confidence in the information, procedures, requirements and recommendations they contain.

Standards are prepared so that individuals, and or statistical organizations can apply the information contained to enhance statistical development. Therefore information presented in a standard, and the language used must be precise and unambiguous, clear to users on what must be done to comply with the standard, and what is optional.

4.1 Standard documentation structure

To ensure uniformity, the following structure is presented to guide National Statistical Systems as they design and document their standards and guidelines. As a reference, this structure has been adopted for documenting National Quality standards for statistics in Uganda.

Figure 2. Standards Documentation Structure and Format

Contents   Page
Foreword
Introduction
1   Scope
2   Conformance
3   Normative references
4   Terms and definitions
5   Symbols (and abbreviated terms)
6   Clause
7   Clause
Annex A (normative) Annex title
A.1 General
A.2 Clause
A.2.1   Subclause (level 1)
A.2.2   Subclause (level 1)
A.3 Clause
Annex B (informative)
Bibliography

5.   NSS Experiences in Standardization

Case 1: Statistics South Africa

For Statistics South Africa to maintain its legislative obligation and to ensure good quality products, it is crucial that the products and their underlying data adhere to relevant standards. To address this, a process of Standards Development within the Standards division was initiated and implemented. This process *(refer to section 2.4)*, provides guiding principles on how standards should be identified, developed, tested, implemented, supported and maintained in Statistics South Africa. It also provides guiding principles for related activities, such as the infrastructure for standards in Statistics South Africa, standards outside of Statistics South Africa (including those within the National Statistical System), and the development of expertise in standards.

So far, a number of standards have been developed. Some of these include; the South African Statistical Quality Assessment Framework (SASQAF) and Concepts and Definitions for Statistics South Africa *(Statistics South Africa, 2017)*.

The Uganda Bureau of Statistics (UBOS) Act of 1998, Section 4 (ii), mandates the Bureau as the lead statistical agency responsible for promoting standardisation in the collection, analysis and publication of statistics to ensure quality, adequacy of coverage and reliability of statistics information. The Bureau is also the lead coordinator and supervisor of Uganda's National Statistical System (NSS). As a result, key data producers in the NSS interface, and are expected to adopt recommended standards, classifications, guidelines and methodologies in their data production processes.

Enabling structures for standardization

i. An inclusive Statistical Legislation & Policy Framework: The UBOS Act (1998) is the prevailing Legislation for statistics in Uganda. The Act underlines the Bureau's responsibility in spearheading standardization for statistics. Similarly, Section 4 (ii) of the Act requires a regulatory framework for statistics produced in the NSS. Requisite statistical guidelines, quality standards, policies and manuals have been designed inline with this legal requirement.

ii. The Plan for National Statistical Development (PNSD). The PNSD provides an overarching Framework for Statistics development in Uganda (Uganda Bureau of Statistics, 2014). As one of its focus areas in the strategic goal on Quality Assurance, standardization is earmarked to enhance credibility of national statistics produced in regard to the quality attributes of integrity, methodological soundness, accuracy and reliability, serviceability and accessibility. Standardization is not only promoted at national level but also at sectoral and local government levels as indicated in the Sector strategic plans for Statistics (*for Ministries, Departments and Agencies*) and Local Government Strategic Plans for Statistics (*for the districts and higher local governments*).

iii. Internationally and Nationally Recommended Guidelines and Best Practices: The UN Fundamental Principles of Official Statistics, UN Guidelines and Compilation manuals, IMF Guidelines, ISO Standards (eg ISO 9000 & 9001 on Quality Management Systems), National Development and Organizational Frameworks have all made provisions for the NSS to deliver high quality statistics and ensure efficiency in statistical production, while minimising duplication of efforts through standardization.

Development of Uganda Standards for Statistics

The need for developing national specific standards for quality statistics was conceived at the PNSD design stage. Stakeholder-wide consultations prompted the Uganda Bureau of Statistics (UBOS) to collaborate with the Uganda National Bureau of Standards (UNBS) in the development process. The UNBS is the mandated body responsible for formulating Uganda Standards. As a result of the development process, 3 Uganda Standards were designed for the National Statistical System. These were formulated through a participatory and consultative process spearheaded by a Standards Technical Committee established by UNBS and chaired by UBOS. The 3 Uganda Standards were later approved for adoption by the National Standards Council for Uganda.

The standards include;

i. ***US 1SO 3534 - Statistics Vocabulary and Symbols (part 1-3)***

An International standard developed by the International Organisation of Standardisation for applied statistics vocabulary and symbols. The standard was adopted as a Uganda Standard, following recommendations of the Standards TC Committee (UNBS TC/17). *The ISO 3534-1:2006: Statistics — Vocabulary and symbols*; is in 3 parts namely; ***Part 1:*** *General statistical terms and terms used in probability,* ***Part 2:*** *Applied statistics and* ***Part 3:*** *Design of experiments*

ii.   US 942: Code of Practice for Official Statistics

A National Quality Standard with a set of guiding principles and practices for ensuring production and dissemination of official statistics in the National Statistical System. The Code defines the criteria and sets basic requirements for designation and certification of official statistics in the country. Therefore, all statistical quality assessments and audit systems in the NSS are aligned with the requirements of this standard. The Code aims to; improve trust and confidence in the independence, integrity and accountability of all statistics produced in the National Statistical System, and promote the application of best international statistical principles, methods and practices to enhance statistical quality.

Figure 4. Principles and Protocols in the US 942

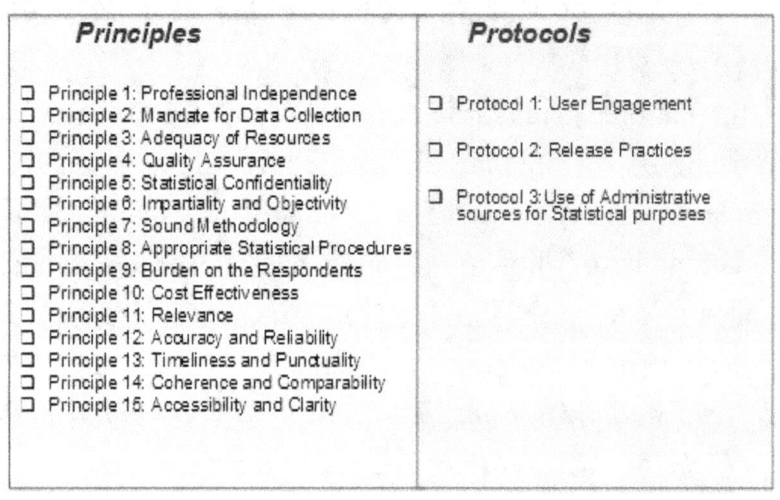

Source: Uganda National Bureau of Standards, 2012

iii.   US 943: Guidelines for Production of Quality Statistics

A national quality standard which ensures all statistical processes and related outputs follow systematic production procedures. While several production processes do exist, The US 943 covers three main production processes through which statistics are primarily produced; these include censuses, ***surveys and administrative data.*** For each process, a set of quality guidelines are provided from the planning of the process to the evaluation stages. To ensure conformity with the national standards, statistical quality assessments and audits are undertaken.

Case 3: European Statistical System & International Systems

In recent years, much work has been going on in the field of quality management and standardization (Eurostat, 2007). Various quality management models and frameworks (like the EFQM model (European Foundation for Quality Management), standards like the ISO 9000, the Data Quality Assessment Framework (DQAF) or the European Statistics Code of Practice) have been advocated for use in the European Statistical System (ESS) member institutions (Eurostat, 2007). While recent literature criticized the "multitude of overlapping quality frameworks" (Statistics Sweden 2006a) and noted that complexity of multidimensional quality approaches could have serious drawbacks for the improvement of quality work (Sæbø, 2006), remarkable implementation efforts in standardization have been undertaken.

The European Statistics Code of Practice consists of 15 principles and 77 indicators. These principles include; Professional Independence, Mandate for Data Collection and Access to Data, Adequacy of Resources, Commitment to Quality, Statistical Confidentiality and Data Protection, Impartiality and Objectivity, Sound Methodology, Appropriate Statistical Procedures, Non-Excessive Burden on Respondents, Cost Effectiveness, Relevance, Accuracy and Reliability, Timeliness and Punctuality, Coherence and Comparability, Accessibility and Clarity (Eurostat, 2017). The principles are partly inspired by Total Quality Management (TQM) and partly cover the nine EFQM quality criteria (e.g. leadership, policy and strategy, people, people results and society results). They also overlap with the ESS quality declaration but the Code of Practice describes a minimum standard whereas the quality declaration is rather a vision. The indicators have been developed for a periodic review of implementation in the ESS, based on a sequence of self-assessments, peer reviews and reports (Eurostat, 2007). Generally, the principles in institutional frameworks, like the European Statistics Code of Practice, can be seen as a general superstructure to all other measures which are later described on the product and process level. They aim at supporting improvement of quality in the organizations as well as enhancing the credibility of the outputs via defining and assessing performance indicators. Special emphasis lies on the assessment of statistical systems and their positive development for international (cooperative) purposes.

The principles integrate a considerable number of (if not all) indicators of statistical products and processes and thus cover the aspects of product and process quality nearly completely (Eurostat, 2007). In theory, all products and processes can be synthesized to a general picture of the respective organization or statistical system. Therefore it should be possible to assign nearly all aspects of process and product quality to one or more principles in the institutional framework, although they are not always mentioned explicitly. Data quality assessment is mentioned in various principles and indicators of the European Statistics Code of Practice. Numerous principles and indicators are only conceivable under the precondition that coherent and well implemented approaches towards data quality assessment are in place. For example, according to principle 7, "adequate tools, procedures and expertise" have to be applied in order to achieve "sound methodology". In order to figure out whether a statistical procedure could be referred to as "adequate", generally accepted assessment methods and tools are required. According to the European Statistics Code of Practice, data quality assessment methods and tools have to provide a complete picture including all steps in the survey process (Eurostat, 2007):

- According to principle 4, the complete production process as well as the entirety of product quality dimensions have to be regularly monitored: it is required that "product quality is regularly monitored", "processes are in place to monitor the quality of the collection, processing and dissemination of statistics" and that there is a "regular and thorough review of the key statistical outputs".

- Monitoring and reviewing survey and sample design as well as fieldwork, data entry, coding, editing and imputation constitute the core of principle 8.
- Principle 11 requires monitoring relevance.
- Principle 12 requires an assessment and validation of the source data as well as statistical outputs, and an assessment of sampling and non-sampling errors.

Quality assurance frameworks that foster standardization have already been developed by several international organizations as well as National Statistical Institutes (NSIs). Examples include Statistics Canada (2002), Statistics Sweden (Bergdahl and Lyberg 2004), the Office for National Statistics of the United Kingdom (ONS), Statistics Norway (Sæbø 2003), the U.S. Census Bureau (Bushery 2004), Eurostat, the Organization of Economic Cooperation and Development (OECD, 2003), and the Australian Bureau of Statistics. As noted by Lindén (2006), quality assurance frameworks encompass the definition of quality requirements for statistical processes and products (as well as some institutional features) and the related quality assessment methods and tools which are to be applied in the organization. In some cases the concrete quality requirements for products and processes are additionally documented in separate quality guidelines (e.g. Statistics Canada, 2003; Statistics Finland, 2003, Statistisches Bundesamt 2006).

The Generic Statistical Business Process Model (GSBPM) developed by United Nations Economic Commission for Europe (UNECE) has been adopted by many statistical organizations and countries implementing the model or a similar one. Defining and mapping business processes in statistical organizations started at least 10 years ago; for example ; the "Statistical value chain" in EU countries, Office for National Statistics (ONS-UK), the "Statistical production cycle" in UBOS, "Business process model"(GSBPM) in South Africa, Statistics New Zealand etc. The GSBPM (UNECE, 2006) provides a standardized approach for statistics production, under different process levels with specific sub-processes and components for each process level (See Annex D for detailed descriptions).

Figure 4. Summary of GSBPM Process levels

The GSBPM provides a practical framework that ensures these processes flow logically and interact systematically to deliver high quality statistical outputs and services. The 9 process levels include, *Specify Needs, Design, Build, Collect, Process, Analyse, Disseminate, Archive and Evaluate (figure 4)*.

6. Integrating IT Innovations in Standardization

Increased adoption of new innovations as a result of standardization is important because rival and incompatible approaches competing in the marketplace can slow or even kill the growth of technology (Shapiro, Carl &Varian, 1999). The shift to a modularized architecture as a result of standardization brings increased flexibility, rapid introduction of new products, and the ability to more closely meet individual customer's needs (Christensen &Raynor, 2003). The negative effects of standardization on technology have to do with its tendency to restrict new technology and innovation. Standards shift competition from features to price because the features are defined by the standard, however, the degree to which this is true depends on the specificity of the standard (Shapiro, Carl &Varian, 1999). Standardization in an area also rules out alternative technologies as options while encouraging others (Cowan, 1991). With regard to statistics, new technologies and communication facilities have sprung up and are reforming the landscape in which statistical systems operate. Recently, the rise of storage capacity and processing power is as staggering and mind boggling as the amounts of raw data available. In order to benefit optimally from these developments, the production ways of statistics should be reconsidered. They should be based on common and standardized processes, transforming raw data into statistical products according to generic and commonly accepted information concepts.

Reusable and modular building blocks are a prerequisite for flexible and cost effective production processes (Braaksma, Colasanti, Falorsi, Kloek, Miguelangel, Vidal, Museux, Szep, 2013).

> *Piet-Hein Daverveldt, Managing Director-Netherlands Standardization Institute (NEN) shared invaluable insights on Standardization and Innovation from the ISO-CERN Conference 13th-14h November 2014, "Standards play a key role in facilitating the market potential of innovative ideas. Standards set the frameworks needed to unleash creativity and force choices. Without standardization, I believe that innovation slows down because legacy systems survive longer. But the most important benefit of standards is that they contribute to the dissemination of knowledge so that others can build on them and improve them further without having to reinvent the wheel".*

OECD (2015) defines innovation as the implementation of new or significantly improved products (goods or services) or processes, a new marketing method, or a new organizational method in business practices, workplace organization or external relations. Worldwide, emerging economies have a stronger role given the increasing speed of technological change impacting global markets. As standards try to keep pace with the interminably faster product development cycles, standardization systems try to adapt to the rapidly evolving environment, facilitating innovation. Hence, standards can support innovation in a number of ways (ISO, 2014);

- Existing standards can codify and spread the state of the art in various technologies, disseminating knowledge, both within and outside the relevant industry community.

- Innovations can more easily gain market acceptance if they comply with existing standards for safety, quality and performance.

- Standards can have an important catalytic role in demand side measures to encourage innovation such as outcome based regulations or public procurement of innovation.

- Standards can help to bridge the gap between research and marketable products or services. A standard can codify the results of publicly funded research, thus making them available as a basis for further innovation. This can be a highly effective mechanism for knowledge and technology transfer.

To demonstrate how Information Technology (IT) is being used as an innovation driver for standardization, best practices are derived from Statistics Canada showcasing how they utilize IT to automate, integrate and actualize their statistics production systems.

> *Statistics Canada (2016), "Successful statistical organizations base their operations on a cost-effective, solution-focused infrastructure that comprises data and information services, processing and analysis capabilities, and the underlying network and computing structure. Information technology (IT) is a strategic enabler of all modernization activities, such as process automation, method innovation, and information- and data-management capabilities. IT modernization is a key component of the Corporate Business Architecture (CBA) transformation initiative carried out by Statistics Canada. IT transformation involves platform standardization, data management, metadata-driven capabilities, and a centralized IT function".*

Statistics Canada has deployed a Common Statistical Production Architecture (CSPA) which brings together existing frameworks and introduces new frameworks related to Statistical Services. The CSPA allows for developing a harmonized top-level description of the "system" of producing statistics aligned with the modernization initiative. In addition, the CSPA gives users an understanding of the different statistical production elements (i.e., processes, information, applications, services) that make up a statistical organization and of how those elements relate to each other. It also emphasizes commonality by providing a common vocabulary with which to discuss implementations. This approach enables the vision and strategy of the statistical industry, by providing a clear, cohesive and achievable picture of what is required to get there (United Nations Economic Commission for Europe, 2015a)

Statistics Canada also uses the Generic Statistical Business Process Model (GSBPM) in the core of its Corporate Business Architecture (CBA) vision. Governance and standardization efforts employ the GSBPM model as an analysis framework to identify possibly redundant applications that may be suitable for elimination. This model also serves to assess the degree to which survey productions areas have migrated to the standard applications, gaps, and plans needed to complete the migration (as directed by CBA). The "Generic Services" component of the CBA focuses on common business activities associated with the Collect, Process, Analyze, and Disseminate elements of the GSBPM. By creating common business units to perform these activities on behalf of all survey areas, this model enables IT to create common solution platforms. Statistics Canada also uses the GSBPM in its application portfolio management work to ensure that survey areas are using common platforms (with exceptions if warranted) and to plan future investment roadmaps. The CBA principles are applied as a basis for governance activities within the organization (Statistics Canada, 2016)

Based on the illustrations and case examples provided, the importance of standards to statistics production cannot be overstated. Likewise, as Hatto (2010) rightly noted, without standards technologically advanced societies could not have developed. More importantly, standards derive their legitimacy from the voluntary and consensual nature of their development process. There is no doubt that without standards the complex, technological world in which we live could not possibly operate.

Final Thoughts.........

Benefits and challenges of standardization have continued to capture the attention of statistical organizations, business and market leaders around the world. Focusing on standardization efforts for quality or innovation, this book draws on research into best practice alternatives which maximize operational excellence. Approaches to developing and implementing standards context-specific to National Statistical Systems, are discussed in view of their benefits as long term strategic initiatives for existing and emerging organizations .If statistical systems and resulting processes are not coordinated in pursuit of standardization goals, the risk of working at cross purpose and high production costs is eminent. But also, it is important to understand that every organization has different needs and resources. As a result, standardization strategies should be developed accordingly.

Further Readings

1. Dickson, E. W.; Singh, S.; Cheung, D. S.; Wyatt, C. C.; & Nugent, A. S. (2008). Application of Lean Manufacturing Techniques in the Emergency Department. *Journal of Emergency Medicine. 37* (2): 177–182. doi:10.1016/j.jemermed.2007.11.108.

2. Langenberg, T. (2005). Standardization and Expectations. Berlin: Springer-Verlag. ISBN 3-540-28112-6.

3. Murphy, C. N.; Yates, J. (2008). The International Organization for Standardization (ISO) : Global Governance Through Voluntary Consensus. New York: Routledge. ISBN 978-0-415-77429-1.

4. Wenzlhuemer, Roland (2010). "The History of Standardisation in Europe". European History Online.

Bibliography

1. Australian Bureau of Statistics (2009). Data Quality Framework, Australia.

2. Braaksma, B; Colasanti, C; Falorsi,P.D; Kloek, W; Miguelangel; Vidal,M; Museux,J.M; & Szep,K. (2013). Standardisation in the European Statistical System. European Commission Statistical Office of the European Union (EUROSTAT).

3. Bergdahl, M. & Lyberg, L. (2004). Quality Management at Statistics Sweden. Current Work and the Future: Paper presented at the European Conference on Quality and Methodology in Official Statistics (Q2004), Mainz, Germany.

4. Blind, K. (2004). The Economics of Standards, Cheltenham: Edward Elgar. ISBN 978 1 84376 793 0.

5. Bower, K.M. (2018). Statistical Process Control. Retrieved from http://asq.org/learn-about-quality/statistical-process-control/overview/overview.html.

6. Bushery, J. M. (2004). How the U.S. Census Bureau Uses the Capability Maturity Model as a Roadmap to Process Improvement. Paper presented at the European Conference on Quality and Methodology in Official Statistics (Q2004), Mainz, Germany.

7. BSI (2010). BSI Group Annual Report and Financial Statements.

8. Cowan, R. (1991). "High Technology and the Economics of Standardization." Paper presented at the International Conference on Social and Institutional Factors Shaping Technological Development: Technology at the Outset, Berlin, Germany, May 27–28, 12-20.

9. Christensen, C.M.; Raynor, M.E. (2003). The Innovator's Solution: Creating and Sustaining Successful Growth. *Harvard Business School Press*, 131-140. Boston.

10. Deming, W. E. (1950). Lectures on statistical control of quality. Nippon Kagaku Gijutsu Remmei.

11. Dyer, C. K; Moseley, P. T; Ogumi, Z; Rand, D. A. J; & Scrosati, B. (2010). Encyclopedia of Electrochemical Power Sources. Newnes, 540. ISBN 9780444527455.

12. European Communities, International Monetary Fund, OECD, United Nations &World Bank (2008). System of National Accounts. Retrieved from https://unstats.un.org/unsd/nationalaccount/docs/SNA2008.pdf.

13. Eurostat(2007). Handbook on Data Quality Assessment Methods and Tools, Eurostat, European Commission. Retrieved from https://unstats.un.org/unsd/dnss/docs-nqaf/Eurostat-Handbook.pdf .

14. Eurostat (2017). European Statistics Code of Practice: For the National Statistical Authorities and Eurostat (EU statistical authority) Retrieved from http://ec.europa.eu/eurostat/documents/4031688/8971242/KS-02-18-142-EN-N.pdf/e7f85f07-91db-4312-8118-f729c75878c7. ISBN 978-92-79-80014-6.

15. Fray, M. (2010).Colonel Crompton: the king of electricity. International Electrotechnical Commission. Retrieved from

http://www.iec.ch/about/history/articles/colonel_crompt on.htm.

16. Gilbert, K. R.; & Galloway, D. F. (1978). Machine Tools. A history of technology. Oxford: Clarendon Press.

17. Hatto, P. (2010). Standards and Standardization Handbook. European Commission. Retrieved from http://www.iec.ch/about/globalreach/academia/pdf/acad emia_governments/handbook-standardisation_en.pdf.

18. ILO (2012). International Standard Classification of Occupations Structure, group definitions and correspondence tables (ISCO-08). Retrieved from http://www.ilo.org/wcmsp5/groups/public/@dgreports/ @dcomm/@publ/documents/publication/wcms_172572. pdf.

19. ISO (2016). How does ISO develop standards? Retrieved from http://www.iso.org/iso/home/standards_development.ht m.

20. Lee, S. (1900). Dictionary of National Biography. LXI. London: Smith Elder.

21. Lindley, D. (2005). Degrees Kelvin: A Tale of Genius, Invention, and Tragedy. National Academic Press, 293. ISBN 978-0309096188.

22. IMF (2014).Government finance Statistics manual. Retrieved from https://www.imf.org/external/Pubs/FT/GFS/Manual/2014/gfsfinal.pdf.

23. International Electrotechnical Commission. (1906). Report of Preliminary Meeting: The minutes from our first meeting. London, 46–47.

24. International Organization for Standardization. (1997). Friendship among equals: Recollections from ISO's first fifty years. 15–18. ISBN 92-67-10260-5.

25. ISO (2014).Standardization and innovation, ISO-CERN conference proceedings. Retrieved from https://www.iso.org/files/live/sites/isoorg/files/archive/pdf/en/standardization_and_innovation.pdf

26. Jenkinson, G. (2006). Standard Quality Reports and their Applications for the National Accounts at the ONS, European Conference on Quality in Survey Statistics (Q2006),

27. Cardiff, United Kingdom.

28. Johnson, J.; Randell, W. (1948). Colonel Crompton and the Evolution of the Electrical Industry. Longman Green.

29. Lindén, H. (2006). First results from the in-depth surveys on quality assurance frameworks and quality reporting. Paper presented at the Conference on Data Quality for International Organizations, Newport, Wales.

30. McWilliam., Robert, C. (2001). BSI: The first hundred years. London: Thanet. ISBN 978-0727730206.

31. OECD (2002). Statistics: Measuring the Non-Observed Economy-A Handbook. Retrieved from http://www.oecd.org/sdd/na/1963116.pdf.

32. OECD (2003). Quality Framework and Guidelines for OECD Statistical Activities. Paris, OECD Document STD/QFS.

33. OECD (2005). Oslo Manual: Guidelines for Collecting and Interpreting Innovation Data.

34. Hatto, P. (2011). A practical guide for researchers. European Commission, Directorate-General for Research & Innovation, Standards and Standardisation.

35. Ping, W. (2011). A Brief History of Standards and Standardization Organizations: A Chinese Perspective, Retrieved from https://www.eastwestcenter.org/system/tdf/private/econ wp117.pdf?file=1&type=node&id=32840.

36. Project Management Institute (2013). A Guide to the Project Management Body of Knowledge (PMBOK Guide). Newtown Square, PA: Project Management Institute. ISBN-13: 978-1935589679.

37. Project Management Institute (2008). A Guide to the Project Management Body of Knowledge (PMBOK Guide). Fourth Edition. Newtown Square, PA: Project Management Institute. ISBN- 978-1-933890-51-7.

38. Rolt, L. T. C. (1962). Great Engineers. Bell and Sons.

39. Statistics Canada, (2009). "A framework for developing Environmental Statistics."

40. Statistics South Africa, (2010), South African Statistical Quality Assessment Framework (SASQAF), edition 2, Statistics South Africa.

41. Statistics South Africa (2017). Standardization: Standards Development Cycle. Retrieved from http://www.statssa.gov.za/?page_id=371.

42. Statistics Canada (2000). Policy on informing Users of Data Quality and Methodology. Statistics Canada.

43. Uganda Bureau of Statistics (2014). Plan for National Statistical Development: Enhancing Data Quality and Use. Kampala, Uganda.

44. Statistics Canada (2003). Statistics Canada's quality guidelines, 4(12-539-XIE).

45. Sæbø, H. V. (2006). Systematic Quality Work in Official Statistics – Theory and Practice. Paper presented at the European Conference on Quality in Survey Statistics (Q2006), Cardiff, United Kingdom.

46. Sæbø, H. V. (2003). Quality Issues at Statistics Norway. Journal of Official Statistics, 19, 287-303.

47. Shapiro, Carl; Varian,H.R. (1999). Information Rules: A Strategic Guide to the Network Economy. Harvard Business School Press, 229-264, Boston.

48. Sidak,J.G.(2016). The Value of a Standard Versus the Value of Standardization. https://www.criterioneconomics.com/the-value-of-a-standard-versus-the-value-of-standardization.html.

49. Statistics Sweden (2006a). Rapporteur Report on Quality Frameworks and the Link with Institutional Frameworks and Principles. Paper presented at the 54th session of the Conference of European Statisticians, Paris, France.

50. Statistics Canada (2002). Statistics Canada's Quality Assurance Framework. Ottawa: Canada.

51. Statistics Canada (2003). Statistics Canada Quality Guidelines. 3rd edition, Ottawa: Canada.

52. Statistics Canada (2016). Modernization of Information Technology and Informatics Services. Retrieved from https://www150.statcan.gc.ca/n1/pub/11-634-x/2016001/section3/chap2-eng.htm.

53. Statistisches Bundesamt (2006).Qualitätsstandards der amtlichen Statistik. Quality Guidelines of Official Statistics. Auflage, Wiesbaden, Statistische Ämter des Bundes und der Länder.

54. Uganda Bureau of Statistics. (1998). UBOS Act, Section 4(2), Republic of Uganda.

55. UNECE. (2009). Generic Statistical Business Process Model. Eurostat, OECD Work Session on Statistical Metadata, UNECE Secretariat. United Nations Economic Commission for Europe, 8–9. Retrieved from http://www.unece.org/stats/gsbpm.

56. Uganda National Bureau of Standards. (2012). Uganda Standard for Statistics, US 942, Code of Practice for Official Statistics.

57. Uganda National Bureau of Standards. (2012). Uganda Standard for Statistics, US 943, Guidelines for Production of Quality Statistics.

58. Uganda National Bureau of Standards. (2012). US ISO 3534-1: Statistics — Vocabulary and symbols — Part 1: General statistical terms and terms used in probability.

59. Uganda National Bureau of Standards. (2012). US ISO 3534-2: Statistics — Vocabulary and symbols — Part 2: Applied Statistics.

60. Uganda National Bureau of Standards. (2012). US ISO 3534-3: Statistics — Vocabulary and symbols — Part 3: Design of experiments.

61. United Nations (2008a). System of National Accounts. European Communities, International Monetary Fund, OECD, United Nations &World Bank. Retrieved from https://unstats.un.org/unsd/nationalaccount/docs/SNA2008.pdf.

62. United Nations (2008b). International Standard Industrial Classification of All Economic Activities (ISIC), Rev 4, Department of Economic and Social Affairs- Statistics Division, Retrieved from https://www.un-ilibrary.org/economic-and-social-development/international-standard-industrial-classification-of-all-economic-activities-isic-rev-4_8722852c-en.

63. United Nations (2015). Central Product Classification (CPC) Version 2.1. Department of Economic and Social Affairs- Statistics Division, Retrieved from

https://unstats.un.org/unsd/classifications/unsdclassificat ions/cpcv21.pdf.

64. United Nations (2000). Classification of Individual Consumption According to Purpose (COICOP). Department of Economic and Social Affairs- Statistics Division. Retrieved from https://unstats.un.org/unsd/publication/SeriesM/SeriesM _84E.pdf.

65. United Nations (2017). Harmonized Commodity Description and Coding Systems (HS). Retrieved from https://unstats.un.org/unsd/tradekb/Knowledgebase/5001 8/Harmonized-Commodity-Description-and-Coding-Systems-HS.

66. UNESCO (2011). International Standard Classification of Education. UNESCO Institute for Statistics. http://uis.unesco.org/sites/default/files/documents/intern ational-standard-classification-of-education-isced-2011-en.pdf.

67. World Health Organisation, 2006, "Framework for developing health-based electromagnetic field standards."

68. Zongjie, X; Hall, J; McCarthy, I.P; Skitmore, M; &
Shen, L (2016). "Standardization efforts: The
relationship between knowledge dimensions, search
processes and innovation outcomes". Technovation.
Innovation and Standardization. 48–49: 69–78.
doi:10.1016/j.technovation.2015.12.002.

Annex A: Template for Standards Implementation Plan

Responsibility Centre	Standards Implementation Tracker					
	Planned strategy to develop Standard/s	Strategic Actions and Tasks	Process Inputs *Budget Estimates (Human, Money, Time, Facilities)*	Expected Deliverables	Timelines Total Implementation period	

Annex B: Fundamental Principles of Official Statistics

The following UN Fundamental Principles for Official Statistics were developed by the Economics and Social Council statistical Commission of the United Nations:

Principle 1: Relevance, impartiality and equal access
Official statistics provides an indispensable element in the information system of a democratic society, serving the Government, the economy and the public with the data about the economic, demographic, social and environmental situation. To this end, official statistics that meet the test of practical utility are to be compiled and made available on an impartial basis to honour citizen's entitlement to public information.

Principle 2: Professional standards and ethics
To retain trust in official statistics, UBOS will decide, according to strictly professional considerations, including scientific principles and professional ethics, on the methods and procedures for the collection, processing, storage and presentation of statistical data.

Principle 3: Accountability and transparency
To facilitate the correct interpretation of data, UBOS will present information according to scientific standards on the sources, methods and procedures of statistics.

Principle 4: Prevention of misuse
UBOS is entitled to comment on erroneous interpretation and misuse of statistics.

Principle 5: Cost-effectiveness
Data for statistical purposes may be drawn from all types of sources, be they statistical surveys or administrative records. UBOS will choose the source with regard to quality, timeliness, costs and the burden on respondents.

Principle 6: Confidentiality
Individual data collected by UBOS and other MDAs for statistical compilation, whether they refer to natural or legal persons, will be strictly confidential and used exclusively for statistical purposes.

Principle 7: Legislation
The laws, regulations and measures under which the statistical systems operate will be made public.

Principle 8: National coordination
UBOS will promote coordination among statistical producers within Uganda in order to advance consistency and efficiency in the National Statistical System.

Principle 9: International standards
UBOS will use international concepts, classifications and methods, where possible, to promote the consistency and efficiency of statistical systems among MDAs.

Principle 10: International cooperation
Bilateral and multilateral cooperation in statistics contributes to the improvement of systems of official statistics in all countries.

Annex C: Standards Profiling Template

Name of Standard (*Edition /Version/ year*)	Purpose	Organization *Firm/Agency /Department Implementing Standard*	Specificity *(Statistics type/category applying standard)*		Use and application *(How and to what extent the standard is used, descriptions for non-application and compliance gaps)*	

Annex D: Generic Statistical Business Process Model

The GSBPM model (UNECE, 2006) descriptions for each of the 9 phases in figure 4 are presented below;

1. Need

The phase describes the development and design activities, and any associated practical research work needed to define the statistical outputs, concepts, methodologies, collection instruments and operational processes. For statistical outputs produced on a regular basis, this phase usually occurs for the first iteration, and whenever improvement actions are identified in phase 9 (Evaluate) of a previous iteration.

1.1 Determine need for information

- Initial investigation and identification of what statistics are needed and what is needed of the statistics.
- Consideration of practice amongst other statistical organizations, and methods used by those organizations.

1.2 Consult and confirm need

- Consulting with the stakeholders and confirming in the detail the need for the statistics. Statistical organizations should know what it is expected to deliver, when, how and perhaps more importantly, why.

- Determining whether previously identified needs have changed. This detailed understanding of user needs is the critical part of this sub-process.

1.3 Establish output objectives

- Identifies the statistical outputs that are required to meet the user needs identified in sub-process 1.2 (Consult and confirm need).
- Agreeing the suitability of the proposed outputs and their quality measures with users.

1.4 Check data availability

- Checks whether current data sources could meet user requirements, and the conditions under which they would be available, including any restrictions on their use.
- Research into potential administrative data sources and their methodologies to determine whether they would be suitable for use for statistical purposes.
- Prepare a strategy for filling any remaining gaps in the data requirements.

1.5 Prepare a business case

- Documents the findings of the other sub-processes in this phase in the form of a business case to get approval to implement the new or modified statistical business process.

- Such a business case would typically include:
  - A description of the " As-Is" business processes (if it already exists), with information on how the current statistics are produced highlighting any inefficiencies and issues to be addressed
  - The proposed "To-Be" solution, determining how the statistical business process will be developed to produce the new or revised statistics;
  - An assessment of costs and benefits, as well as any external constraints.

2. Design

The phase describes development and design activities, and any associated practical research work needed to define the statistical outputs, concepts, methodologies, collection instruments and operational processes. For statistical outputs produced on a regular basis, this phase usually occurs for the first iteration, and whenever improvement actions are identified in phase 9 (evaluate) of a previous iteration.

2.1 outputs

- Contains the detailed design of the statistical outputs to be produced including the related development work and preparation of the system and tools used in the disseminate phase.
- Outputs should be designed, wherever possible, to follow existing standards, so inputs to this process may include metadata from similar or previous collections, international standards and information

about practices in other statistical organizations from sub-process determine need for information.

2.2 Frame and sample methodology

- Identifies and specifies the population of interest, defines a sampling frame (and, where necessary, the register from which it is derived), and determines the most appropriate sampling criteria and the methodology (which could include complete enumeration). Common sources are administrative and statistical registers, censuses and sample surveys.

- Describes how these sources can be combined if needed

- Analysis of whether the frame covers the target population should be performed

- A sampling plan should be made: the actual sample is created in sub-process 3.6 (draw sample), using the methodology specified in this sub-process.

2.3 Tabulation Plan/ variables

- Defines the variables to be collected via the data collection instrument, as well as any other variables that will be derived from them in sub-process 5.6 (derive new variables), and any classification that will be used. It is expected that the existing national and international standards will be followed wherever possible.

This may need to run in parallel with sub-process 2.4 (data collection) as the definition of the variables to be collected, and the choice of data collection instrument may be interdependent to some degree.

♦ Preparation of metadata descriptions of collected and derived variables and classification is a necessary precondition for subsequent phases.

2.4 Data collection

♦ Determines the most appropriate data collection method (s) and instrument (s). The actual activities in the sub-process vary according to the type of collection instrument required, which can include computers, assisted interviewing, paper questionnaires, administrative data interfaces and data integration techniques.

♦ Design of questions and response templates (in conjunction with the variables and classifications designed in sub-process 2.3 (tabulation plan/variables))

♦ Design of any formal agreements relating to data supply, such as memoranda of understanding and confirmation of the legal basis for the data collection.

♦ This sub-process is enabled by tools such as questions libraries (to facilitate the reuse of questions and related attributes), questionnaire tools (to enable the quick and easy compilation of questions) into formats suitable for cognitive testing and agreement templates (to help standardize terms and conditions).

♦ Design of process-specific provider management systems.

2.5 Statistical Processing Methodology

♦ Designs the statistical processing methodology to be applied during phase 5 (process), and phase 6 (Analyse).

♦ This can include developing and testing routines for coding, editing, imputing, estimating, integrating, verifying and finalizing datasets.

2.6 Define archive rules

This sub-process is where the archiving rules for the statistical data and metadata resulting from a statistical business process are determined. The requirement to archive intermediate outputs such as the sample file, the raw data from the collect phase, and the results of various stages of the process and the analyse phases should also be considered. The archive rules for a specific statistical business process may be fully or partly dependant on the more general archiving policy of the statistical organization, or, for national organizations, on standards applied across the government sector.

The rules should include consideration of the medium and location of the archive, as well as the requirement for keeping duplicate copies. They should also consider the conditions (if any) under which data and metadata should be disposed of. (Note- this sub-process is logically strongly linked to phase 2-Design, at least for the first iteration of a statistical business process).

2.7 Processing systems and work flow

Determines the workflow from data collection to archiving, taking an overview of all the processes required within the whole statistical process, and ensuring that they fit together efficiently with no gaps or redundancies. Various systems and databases are needed through out the process. However, given the vartious processes and technology across many statistical business processes, existing systems and databases should be examined first, to determine whether they are fit for the purpose of a specific process. In case any gaps are identified, new solutions should be designed.

2.8 Detailed project plan

Develop a project plan giving details on activities to be carried out, start date and the duration of each activity; and human resources allocated to each activity.

This phase builds and tests the production systems to the point where they are ready for use in the "live" environment. For statistical outputs produced on a regular basis, this phase usually occurs for the first iteration, and the following a review or a change in methodology, rather than for every iteration. It is broken down into 5 sub—processes, which are generally sequential, from left to right, but can also occur in parallel, and can be iterative.

3.1   Data collection instrument

♦ Describes the activities to build the collection instruments to be used during the phase 4 (collect). The collection instrument is generated or built based on the design specifications crcatcd during phase 2 (design). A collection may use one or more collections modes to receive the data, e.g. personal or telephone interviews; paper, electronic or web questionnaires. Collection instruments may also be data extraction routines used to gather data from existing statistical or administrative data sets.

♦ Preparing and testing contrasts and functioning of that instrument, (e.g. testing the questions in the questionnaire). It is recommended to consider the direct connection of collection instruments to that statistical metadata system, so that metadata can be more easily captured in the collection phase.

Connection of metadata and data at that point of capture can save work in data phases.

3.2   Process components

♦ Describe the activities to build new and enhance existing software component needed for the business process, as designed in phase 2. (Design). Components may include dashboard functions and features, data repositories, transformation tools, workflow framework components, provider and metadata management tools.

3.3   Configure workflows

♦ Configures the workflow, systems and transformations used within the statistical business processes, from data collection right through to archiving the final statistical output. It ensures that the workflow specified in sub-process 2.7 (processing system and workflow) works in practice.

3.4   Test end-to-end

♦ Describes the activities to manage a field test or pilot of the statistical business process. Typically it includes a small scale data collection, to test collection instruments, followed by processing and analysis of the collected data to ensure, the statistical business process performed as expected.

- Following the pilot, it may be necessary to go back to a previous step and make adjustments to instruments, systems or components. For a major statistical process, e.g. a population census, there may be several iterations until the process is working satisfactorily.

3.5   Finalise production system

Include activities to put the process, including workflow systems, modified and newly-built components in to production ready for use by business areas. The activities include:

- Production documentation about the process components, including technical documentation and uscr manuals.
- Training the business user on how to operate the process.
- Moving the process components in to the production environment and ensuring they work as expected in that environment.

3.6   Draw sample

- Establishes the frame and selects the sample for this iteration of the collection, as specified in sub-process 2.2 (Frame and sample methodology).

♦ Includes the coordination of samples between instances of the same statistical business process (for to manage overlap or rotation),and between different processes using a common frame or register (for example to manage overlap or to spread response burden).Quality assurance, approval and maintenance of the frame and the selected sample are also undertaken in the sub-process, though maintenance of underlying registers, from which frames for several statistical business processes are drawn, is treated as a separate business process.

♦ The sampling aspects of this sub-process is not usually relevant for processes based entirely on the use pre-existing data sources (e.g. administrative data) as such processes generally create frames from the available data and then follow a census approach.

4. Collect

This phase collects all necessary data, using different collection modes (including extractions from administrative and statistical registers and databases), and loads them in to the appropriate data environment. For statistical outputs produced regularly, this phase occurs in each iteration.

4.1 Set up collection

- ◆ Ensures that the people, processes and technology are ready to collect data, in all modes as designed. It takes place over a period of time, as it includes the strategy, planning and training activities in preparation for the specific instance of the statistical business process. Where the process is repeated regularly, some (of all) of these activities may not be explicitly required for each iteration. For one-off and new processes, these activities can be lengthy.

This sub-process includes:

o Preparing a collection strategy.

o Training collection staff

o Ensuring collection resources are available e.g. laptops

o Configuring collection systems to request and receive the data;

o Ensuring the security of data to be collected and Preparing collection instruments (*e.g. printing questionnaires, pre-filling them with exiting data, loading questionnaires and data into interviewers' computers etc.*).

4.2 Run collection

o This is where the collection is implemented, with the different collection instruments being used to collect the data. It includes the initial contact with producers in any subsequent follow-up or reminder actions.

o It records when and how the providers were contacted, and whether they have responded.

o This includes the management of the providers involved in the current collection, ensuring that the relationship between the statistical organization and data providers remains positive, and recording to comments, queries and complaints.

o For administrative data, this process is brief; the provider is either contacted to send the data, or sends it as scheduled. When the collection meets its targets.

4.3   Load data into processing environment

This stage involves initial validation, and loading collected data and metadata into a suitable electronic environment for further processing in phase 5 (process). It may include automatic data take-on, for example using optical character recognition tools to extract data from paper questionnaires, or converting the formats of data files received from other organizations. In cases where there is a physical data collection instrument, such as a paper questionnaire, which is not needed for further processing, this sub-process manages the archiving of that material in conformance with the principles established in phase 8 (Archive).

5. Process

This phase describes the cleaning of data records and their preparation for analysis. It is made up of sub-processes that check, clean, and transform the collected data, and may be repeated several times.

For statistical outputs produced regularly, this phase occurs in each iteration. The sub-processes in this phase can apply to data from both statistical and non-statistical sources (with the possible exception of sub-process 5.7(calculate weights), which is usually specific to survey data).

5.1   Standardize and Anonymise

- o This is where statistical units are derived or standardized, and where data are anonymised.
- o Depending on the type of source data, this sub-process may not always be needed.
- o Standardisation includes converting administrative or collection units into the statistical units required for further processing.
- o Anonymisation strips data of identifiers such as name and address, to help to protect confidentiality. Standardisation and anonymisation may take place before or after sub-process 5.2 (integrate data), depending on the requirements for units and identifiers in that sub-process.

5.2   Integrate data

- ♦ Integrates one or more data sources. The input data can be from the mixture of external or internal data sources, and a variety of collection modes. The results is a harmonized data set. Data integration typically includes;
    - o Matching/ record linkage routines, with the aim of linking data from different sources referring to the same unit;

- o Prioritizing when two or more sources contain data for the same variable (with potentially different values).
- ◆ Data integration may take place at any point in this phase, before or after any of the other sub-processes used. There may also be several instances of data integration in any statistical business process.

5.3   Classify and code

Classifies and codes the input data. For example automatic (or clerical) coding routines may assign numeric codes to text responses according to a pre-determined classification scheme.

5.4   Edit and impute

This applies to collected micro-data, and looks at each record to try to identify (any where necessary correct) missing data, errors and discrepancies. It can also be referred to as input data validation. It may be run iteratively, validating data against predefined edit rules, usually in a set order.

It may apply automatic edits, or raise alerts for manual inspection and correction of the data. Where data are missing or unreliable, estimates are imputed, often using a rule-based approach. *Specific steps include:*

- o The identification of potential errors and gaps; The selection of data to include or exclude from editing and imputation routines;
- o Editing and imputation using one or more predefined methods e.g "hot-deck" or "cold-deck"

- o Imputation and Writing the edited/ imputed data back to the data set, and flagging them as edited or imputed;
- o The production of metadata on the editing and imputation process; Editing and imputation can apply to unit records both from surveys and administrative sources, before and after integration.

5.5   Derive new variables

The sub-process creates variables that are not explicitly provided in the collection and are needed to deliver the required outputs. It derives these new variables by applying arithmetic formulae to one or more of the variables by applying arithmetic formulae to one or more of the variables that are already present in the dataset. It may need to be iterative, as some derived variables may themselves be based on other derived variables. It is therefore important to ensure that variables are derived in correct order.

5.6   Calculate weights

This sub-process creates weights for unit data records according to the methodology created in sub-process 2.5: statistical processing methodology. These weights can be used to "gross-up" sample survey results to make them representative of the target population, or to adjust for non-response in total enumerations.

6. Analyse

In this phase, statistics are produced, examined in detail, interpreted, and made ready for dissemination. This phase includes the sub-processes and activities that enable statistical analysts to understand the statistics produced. For statistical outputs produced regularly, this phase occurs in every iteration. The Analyse phase and sub-processes are generic for all statistical outputs, regardless of how the data were sourced.

6.1   Acquire ancillary information

This sub-process includes many on-going activities involved with the gathering of intelligence, with the cumulative effect of building a body of knowledge about a specific statistical domain. This knowledge is then applied to the current collection, in the current environment, to allow informed analyses. Acquiring a high level of domain intelligence will allow the statistical analyst to understand the data better, and to identify where results might differ from expected values. This allows better explanations of these results in sub-process 6.5 (describe and explain).

6.2   Calculate aggregates

The sub-process creates aggregate data and population totals from micro-data. It includes summing data for records sharing certain characteristics, determining measures of average and dispersion, and applying weights from sub-process 5.6 to sample survey data to derive population totals.

6.3   Prepare draft outputs

The sub-process is where domain intelligence is applied to the data collected to produce statistical outputs. It includes the production of additional measurement such as indices or seasonally adjusted series, as well as the recording of quality characteristics.

6.4   Validate

This sub-process is where statisticians verify the quality of outputs produced, in accordance with a general quality framework. Verification activities can include:

- o Checking that the population coverage and response rates are as required;
- o Comparing the statistics with previous cycles (if applicable);
- o Confronting the statistics against other relevant data (both internal and external);
- o Investigating inconsistencies in statistics;
- o Performing macro-editing;
- o Verifying the statistics against expectations and domain intelligence.

6.5   Describe and explain

This sub-process is where in depth understanding of the outputs is gained by statisticians. They use that understanding to interpret and explain the statistics produced for this cycle by assessing how well the statistics reflect initial expectations, in view of all perspectives using different tools and media, and also while carrying out in depth statistical analyses.

6.6   Disclosure control and anonymise

This sub-process ensures that the data (and the metadata) to be disseminated do not breach the appropriate rules or confidentiality. This may include checks for primary and secondary disclosure, as well as the application of the data suppression or perturbation techniques.

6.7   Finalize outputs for dissemination

This sub-process ensures that statistics and associated information are fit for purpose and reach the required quality level, and are thus ready for dissemination. It includes:
- o   Completing consistency checks;
- o   Determining the level of release, and applying caveats;
- o   Collating support information, including interpretation, briefing, measures of uncertainty and, any other necessary metadata;
- o   Producing the supporting internal documents;
- o   Pre-release discussion with appropriate internal subject matter experts
- o   Approving the statistical content for release.

7. Dissemination

This phase manages the release of the statistical products to customers. For statistical outputs produced regularly, this phase occurs in each iteration. It is of five sub-processes, which are generally sequential, from left to right, but can also occur in parallel, and can be iterative.

7.1   Update output systems

This sub-process manages the update of systems where data and metadata are stored for dissemination purpose, including:

- o Formatting data and metadata ready to be put into output database;
- o Loading data and metadata into output database;
- o Ensuring data are linked to relevant metadata

Note: formatting, loading and linking of metadata should preferably mostly take place in earlier phases, but this sub-process includes a check that all of the necessary metadata are in place and ready for dissemination.

7.2   Produce products

This sub-process produces the products, as previously designed, to meet user needs. The products can take many forms including printed publication, press release and web sites. Typical steps include:

- o Preparing the product components (text, tables, charts etc);
- o Assembling the components into products; & Editing the products and checking that they meet publication standards.

7.3 Produce 'quality statements'

This sub-process produces a quality report. This is a metadata required to declare the quality of a statistical product. This type of metadata should be documented according to the standard template for quality declaration.

7.4 Manage release of products

This sub-process ensures that all elements of the release are in place including managing the timing of the release. It includes briefings specific groups such as the press or ministers, as well as the arrangements for any pre-release embargoes. It also includes the provision of products to subscribers.

7.5 Market and promote products

Whilst marketing in general can be considered to be an over-arching process, this sub-process concern the active promotion and marketing of the statistical products produced in a specific statistical business process, to help them reach the widest possible audience.

It includes the use of customer relationship management tools, to better target potential users of the product, as well as the use of tools including web site, to facilitate the process of communicating statistical information to users.

7.6   Manage customer queries

This sub-process ensures that customer queries are recorded and that responses are provided within agreed deadlines. These queries should be regularly reviewed to provide an input to the over arching quality management process as they can indicate new or changing user needs.

8 Archive

This phase manage the archiving and disposal of statistical data and metadata. Given the reduced costs of data storage, it is possible that the archiving strategy adopted by a statistical organization does not include provision for disposal, so the final sub-process may not be relevant for all statistical business processes. In other cas4es, disposal may be limited to intermediate files from previous iterations, rather than disseminated data.

8.1   Manage archive repository

This sub-process concerns the management of one or more archive repositories. These may be databases, or may be physical locations where copies of data or metadata are stored. It includes:

- o Maintaining catalogues of data and metadata archives, with sufficient information to ensure that individual data or metadata sets can be easily retrieved;
- o Testing retrieval processes;

- o Periodic checking of the integrity of archived data and metadata;
- o Upgrading software-specific archive formats when software changes.

The sub-process may cover a specific statistical business process or a group of processes, depending on the degree of standardization within the organization. Ultimately it may even be considered to be an over-arching process if organization-wide standards are put in place.

8.2 Preserve data and associated metadata

This sub-process is where the data and metadata from a specific statistical business process are archived. It includes:

- o Identifying data and metadata for archiving in line with the rules defined in 8.1;
- o Formatting those data and metadata for the repository;
- o Loading or transferring data and metadata;
- o Cataloguing the archived data and metadata;
- o Verifying that the data and metadata have been successfully archived.

8.3 Dispose of data and associated metadata

This sub-process is where the data and metadata from a specific statistical business process are disposed of. It includes;

- o Identifying data and metadata for disposal, in line with the rules defined in 8.1;
- o Disposal of those data and metadata;

- o Recording that those data and the metadata have been disposed of.

9. Evaluate

This phase manages the evaluation of a specific instance of a statistical business process. It logically takes place at the end of the instance of the process, but relies on inputs gathered throughout the different phases. For statistical output produced regularly, evaluation should at least in theory occur for each iteration, determining whether further iteration should take place, and if so, whether any improvements should be implemented. However, in some cases, particularly for regular and well established statistical business processes, evaluation may not be formally carried out for each iteration. In such cases, this phase can be seen as providing the decision as to whether the next iteration should start from phase 1 (special needs) or from some later phase (often phase 4(collect)).

9.1   Gather inputs for programme review/ evaluation

Evaluation material can be produced in any other phase or sub-process. It may take many forms, including feedback from users, process metadata, and system metrics and staff suggestions. Reports of progress against an action plan agreed during a previous iteration may also form an input to evaluations of subsequent iterations. This sub-process gathers all of these inputs, and makes them available for the person or team producing the evaluation.

9.2   Prepare evaluation report

This sub-process analyses the evaluation inputs and synthesizes them into an evaluation report. The resulting report should note any quality issues specific to this iteration of the statistical business process, and should make recommendations for changes if applicable.

These recommendations can cover changes to any phase or sub-process for future iterations of the process, or can suggest that the process is not repeated.

9.3   Quality plan

This sub-process brings together the necessary decision-making power to form and agree an action plan based on the evaluation report. It should also include consideration of mechanism for monitoring the impact of those actions, which may in-turn; provide an input to evaluations of further iterations of the process.

9.4   Quality management

This process is applies across the entire model. It is closely linked to phase 9 (evaluate), which has the specific role of evaluating individual instances of a statistical business process. The overarching quality management process, however, has a deeper and a broader scope. As well as evaluating iterations of a process, it is also necessary to evaluate separate phases and sub-processes, ideally each time are applied, but at least according to an agreed schedule. These evaluations can apply within a specific process, or across several processes that use common components.

9.5   Metadata management

Good metadata management is essential for the different operation of statistical business processes. Metadata are present in every phase, either created or carried forward from a previous phase. The key challenge is to ensure that they are captured as early as possible, and stored and transferred from phase to phase alongside the data they refer to. A metadata management strategy and IT system (s) are therefore vital to the operation of this model.

Annex E: Towards a Standardized Metadata System

Statistical metadata (descriptive information about the statistics), plays a fundamental role in managing, unifying and standardizing workflows and statistical production processes at organizational, sectoral and national levels. The statistical metadata template and structure in the presented in figure 7 below, draws key components from the online EURO-SDMX Metadata Structure (ESMS) 2.0. It outlines a basic structure and common framework for compiling and maintaining descriptions about the statistics produced within a National Statistical System (NSS). Metadata helps statistics users understand better, what the numbers mean. Therefore, the foundation of an effective statistical metadata system is to identify and document all users, understand their needs and regularly update them on changes (if any) in the metadata. Figure 5 illustrates a practical format and template for statistical metadata.

Figure 5. Statistical Metadata System-- *Template and Structure*

Serial No	Concept Name	Concept Code	Descriptions
Contact	Organization details		
Metadata Update			
1.	Name (Statistic/s produced)		
2.	Unit of Measure		
3.	Scope and coverage		
4.	Source of data		
5.	Statistical Confidentiality		
6.	Data collection, Compilation and Computation methods		
7.	Statistical Processing		
8.	Reference Period for statistics produced		
9.	Release Policy		
10.	Frequency of Dissemination		
11.	Data Revision		
12	Dissemination Format		
Quality Attributes			
13.	Institutional Environment for statistics produced		
14.	Relevance		
15.	Accuracy and reliability		
16.	Timeliness and punctuality		
17.	Comparability		
18.	Coherence		
19.	Accessibility and availability of statistics produced		
20.	Comments and Limitations Log		